Clothespin Cuties

Theresa Hutnick

How cute can a
Cutie get?

The clothespin dolls on the front of this book are just waiting
for you to turn them into your very own Cuties!

Everything you need is right in the book.

Have a grown-up help you make your first Cutie.
Then you can try making one on your own!

How to Make
a Princess

What you'll need
(It's all here in the book.)

- clothespin · long purple yarn
- pink and yellow petal · short light yellow yarn
- short fuzzy blond yarn · sequins
- punch-outs (page 15) · glue

1

Glue one end of the purple
yarn to the back of the
clothespin near the neck.

2

Wrap the yarn around
and down the clothespin.

Glue the end in place.

3

Slide the pink and yellow
petal up from the feet to
the waist.

Add dots of glue under the
petal, front and back.

4 Flip petal down and press in at the waist (where the glue is).

5 Glue light yellow yarn onto the back for arms.

6 Glue the blond fuzzy yarn on the head for hair.

Decorate! Dot drops of glue wherever you wish to add sequins or punch-outs.

Tip:

Let your Cutie sit for at least 15 minutes so the glue can dry.

Make a stand for your Cutie

1 Choose the castle stand from the punch-out page. Fold along scores.

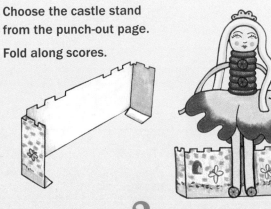

2 Glue your Cutie to the stand.

7

How to Make
a Ballerina

What you'll need
(It's all here in the book.)

· clothespin · long pink yarn ·
orange petal · short tan yarn ·
· short fuzzy brown yarn ·
· sequins · punch-outs (page 15) ·
· glue ·

glue

net wt. .17 oz
5ml

The Ballerina follows
the same steps
as the Princess but
uses a different petal
and yarns.

How to Make
a Mermaid

What you'll need

(It's all here in the book.)

- clothespin -
- long lavender and blue yarn -
- green petal - short light yellow yarn -
- short fuzzy green yarn -
- punch-outs (page 15) -
- sequins - glue -

1

Glue one end of the yarn to the back of clothespin at the waist.

2

Wrap the yarn around and down the clothespin until you end at the ankles. Glue the end in place.

Tip:

If the yarn is too long, just snip with scissors.

3

Slide the green petal over the head to the waist. Add dots of glue under the petal, front and back.

4

Flip petal down and press in at the waist (where the glue is).

5

Glue peach yarn onto the back for arms.

6

Glue the green fuzzy yarn on the head for hair.

Decorate! Dab drops of glue wherever you wish to add sequins or punch-outs. Then let the Cutie dry for at least 15 minutes.

Decorate your
Cuties with pretty
punch-outs!

Just pop them out and
glue onto Cuties.

To make custom Cuties

use items you can find around your house.

- yarn • fancy threads • embroidery floss • ribbons •
- buttons • beads and sequins • felt • feathers •

More Great

Chicken Socks. Books

★ Crayon Rubbings ★ Paper Purses ★ Hand Art ★

★ How to Make Pompom Animals ★ Make Your Own Twirly Tutu ★

★ Make Your Own Twinkly Tiaras ★ Magic Painting ★

★ Tree House Bugs ★ Paper Flowers ★

★ The Super Scissors Book ★

★ Utterly Elegant Tea Parties ★

Can't get enough? Here are some simple ways to keep the Klutz coming.

1 **Order more of the supplies** that came with this book at klutz.com. It's quick, it's easy and, seriously, where else are you going to find this exact stuff?

2 Get your hands on a copy of **The Klutz Catalog.** To request a free copy of our mail order catalog, go to klutz.com/catalog.

3 Become a **Klutz Insider** and get e-mail about new releases, special offers, contests, games, goofiness and who-knows-what-all. If you're a grown-up who wants to receive e-mail from Klutz, head to klutz.com/insider.

If any of this sounds good to you, but you don't feel like going online right now, just give us a call at 1-800-737-4123. We'd love to hear from you.